MW00567895

ISBN 1-882626-13-3

9 781882 626137

90000

A Mother's Kiss

by Anita K. Nobles and Jean Ward-Jones

Impressions Ink • 5147 Patrick Henry Dr. • Memphis, TN 38134
United States • Library of Congress • ISBN 1-882626-13-3

Impressions Ink books are available at your local bookstore or giftstore. For information on the retailers in your area or to place an order please contact:
Impressions Ink • 5147 Patrick Henry Dr. • Memphis, TN 38134
(901) 388-5382 • (800) 388-5382

Printed in the United States of America

Introduction

Life has a way of duplicating itself. Sometimes
I find that I have been duplicated in my daughter – good
natured, thoughtful, hard-headed and quick tempered. On a
daily basis I share with her lessons learned from my own
life. She's a first-grader and, frankly, these tested truths and
wisdoms often go right over her head.

Some of these lessons I had to learn more than once,
being hard-headed. A few of these lessons I watched others
learn the hard way. They are all valuable and I wish that my

3

mother could have passed them on to me but she died when I was fourteen. To be certain these lessons are passed on to my daughter, I've collected them inside this book.

I have been fortunate to have the support and love of family and friends and their strength and wisdom helped turn a negative event into a positive influence. Jean Ward-Jones is one of these people. She's my Mom. Jean married my Dad and that alone would make her special but she's my Mom because she united a fractured family and inspired us to grow into a loving, supportive unit.

I called Jean when I started this book. She helped me to take emotional feelings and thoughts and put them into words. Jean is a communicator and a writer, my Mom, and along with my daughter – one of my best friends.

We wrote this book together in the hope that you will find a valuable thought or a message – a lesson you <u>don't</u> have to learn the hard way. Perhaps you will find words here to express some of your own ideas about living a rewarding and happy life. Feel free to add to this book; we have reserved a blank page in the back for your own special messages. Maybe someone else you know could benefit from both our messages.

We don't expect this small book to change the world but if it helps someone feel less alone, more guided, more confident and more capable we'll be a very happy Mother-Daughter pair.

Dedicated in Memory to
Shirley Ann LeMay Jones
and to those who mothered me in her absence:
Penny Gant, Anne Nobles, Marie G. Jones and Jean Ward-Jones

Turn off the music. Turn off the television. Turn on your imagination and dream impossible dreams.

Figure out how much money you need to live the life you want to live and equip yourself with the education and tools to meet your financial needs.

You're more fortunate than others. Give something back.

Riches come from the love of family and friends – not from bank accounts.

Ask for your fair share but respect the needs of others.

Care for the earth. It will be home for your children.

Competing with others means winning or losing; competing with yourself means improvement.

Some people won't like you.

Learn to appreciate the arts.

Don't do anything that will make you feel bad about yourself later.

Many successful people succeed because they are afraid to fail.

Don't let today's mistakes travel into tomorrow.

Exercise – both mind and body.

Knowing what you want from life makes
it easier to find.

Choose your leaders from people you respect and admire.

Being a woman only limits your options if you let it.

Never let others make you feel guilty. But if your guilt is self-imposed and deserved, change your behavior – and you may need to make some apologies.

Study the sciences; understand the world you live in.

Don't hurt others on purpose; don't let others hurt you.

The more you know about people in other countries, the more accepting you'll be of their differences.

Do good deeds – anonymously.

Know your strengths and use them.

Count what you're given, not what
you give.

Love is only blind when your eyes
are shut.

Speak up but think first.

Help the helpless.

Your shyness will disappear when you help others overcome theirs.

Anything worth having is worth waiting for. The wait may take work.

Love one man at a time.

Dress to be remembered – with controlled flair.

Push yourself beyond your limits and your limits will disappear.

Life is the trip – not the destination.

Hard work pays.

Don't try to do everything yourself. Ask for help and give those who love you an opportunity to demonstrate their love.

You are loved unconditionally, always and regardless.

Spend time with your family and friends – their love will keep you warm on the coldest day.

There are unseen benefits for being nice when others aren't.

If you're talking you can't listen; and you can't learn without listening.

Get a degree in living. Don't let life's lessons pass you by.

Say your prayers, but don't expect God to do all the work.

A bad day makes you appreciate a good one.

If you always do what you've always done, you'll always get what you've always gotten.

Nobody can look after your interests
better than you.

If you ask questions and seek change,
you will find order in the midst of chaos.

Take time to smell the roses.

An occasional cry is healthy.

There is nothing you can't accomplish if you are willing to work hard enough to get it.

When everything seems like an earth-shaking event, postpone decisions until reality sets in.

Self-confidence prevents jealousy.

There is no courage without fear.

Accept responsibility for the
consequences of your actions.

People just want to be loved and accepted. You have the power to give them what they want.

Be as quick to congratulate yourself as to criticize yourself.

Nobody's perfect – thank goodness.

No one is ever as hard on you as you are on yourself.

You only get one body. Learn to like it and take care of it.

Your reputation is important. It speaks for you in your absence.

Finding romantic love is never better than when you weren't looking for it.

When you lose your temper, your self-control goes with it.

You need both male and female friends.

Women can send flowers to men.

Never run from the test.

"What do you think?" – the most important question you can ask.

Don't let finding a mate be your only goal in life.

Ignore those who say "it can't be done" – just go ahead and do it.

When someone hands you a business card, show your interest and respect by reading it.

Don't let a "first impression" cloud your judgment.

Making a good first impression is doing it right the first time.

Gossip tells you more about the person talking than the person talked about.

Just when you think you have all the answers, the questions will change.

Don't mistake an acquaintance for a friend.

If you know where you're going, you'll know when you're off course.

Say no when you want to say no.

True beauty comes from within.

Never stop learning.

Be good to your body. Treat it as if it has to last a lifetime.

Don't volunteer for everything.

Seek opinions and advice from people you admire.

Be honest. Be frank. Be diplomatic. And try to be all three at the same time.

Money and beauty alone are no match for determination and preparation.

If you must borrow money from friends or family, repay them as faithfully as you would repay the bank.

Don't spend more than you have.

Show consideration for others and set the example.

Saving your money <u>increases</u> your options.

Learn to shake hands properly.

Understanding compound interest <u>multiplies</u> your options.

Life won't always be fair.

Do everything you do to the best of your ability and then be proud of what you've done.

Don't follow anyone's advice unless
you're sure it's right for you.

Spend your time wisely. You can't get
a refund.

Do what you say you'll do. Nothing is more important than being true to your word.

Don't gossip. And when others do, don't be swayed by what they say. Form your own conclusions and try to base them on fact, not gossip.

Don't be envious of others. Become someone others will admire.

The greatest reward is being proud of your work.

Go with the flow when you can. You're entitled to an occasional smooth ride.

Take pride in your successes.

Treat others the way you want them to treat you.

You can't be the "center of attention" all the time.

Support your family and friends in their endeavors.

Never date married men.

Enjoy being the center of attention but always be ready to share the spotlight.

Be proud of your feminity – wear it with dignity.

When you stumble and fall, get up and dust yourself off.

If you can't be honest with yourself, how can you be honest with others?

"Love at first sight" happens everyday. Ask any mother how she felt when her baby was first put in her arms.

If you are to succeed, you must first learn to fail.

You'll find only comfort with those who agree with you. You'll find growth with those who don't.

When you need a helping hand, never forget your own.

Do at least one thing everyday to improve yourself.

Never be angry with people for not doing things you didn't ask them to do.

"I've always done it this way" is never an excuse for not doing it better.

Plenty of rest, lots of water and a smile can do more for your complexion than any miracle cream or lotion.

Two secrets of success are thinking ahead and evaluating your options.

Thank God.

All the money in the world cannot buy peace of mind.

The price of quitting is failure.

There are more nice people than mean people, but the mean ones get the most publicity.

If you like yourself, chances are good that others will like you too.

Love people and use things; avoid those who love things and use people.

There are two kinds of failures – those who thought but never did and those who did but never thought.

The most important step in correcting a mistake is admitting it.

You'll never need more strength than you have.

Humor is the best formula for solving problems.

Money solves financial problems – not personal problems.

Happiness comes from helping others yet never forgetting to take care of your own needs as well.

You'll get the heartiest laughs when you laugh at yourself.

Sometimes the best thing to say is nothing.

You can't have your way all the time.

Don't take everything seriously. Just a little humor makes life a lot more fun.

Think before you act and you'll be less likely to regret your actions.

Listen to your intuition; it hears what is not said and sees what is not revealed.

Time heals all wounds.

Practice now what you want to do
well later.

You are responsible for your own
happiness.

People can hurt you only as much as you let them.

See the world.

Marry for love.

Don't follow all the time.

Choose your mate; don't simply be chosen.

Nothing beats preparation.

Smiling increases your face value.

Set goals and write them down. Goals on paper become accomplishments.

Do what makes you happy.

Cultivate friends who are different
from yourself.

Treat yourself the same way you'd treat your best friend – with respect, admiration and love.

Read, read, read.

The difference between bad luck and good luck is perspective.

Act like you know where you're going and others will follow you.

Be careful what you wish for – you may get it.

No one deserves to be abused.

You are worthy of praise. Accept it with a simple "thank you".

You don't have to be a magician to turn negatives into positives.

You can't control Life. But you can prepare for the challenges, disappointments and celebrations it offers.

You only have a few good friends in your whole life. Treat them special.

Don't be satisfied with what's within your reach.

Start your own celebration board. Post pictures of your successes and magazine pages that represent your dreams. Visualize yourself doing the things you want to do. Look at this board often and dream.

Learn a second language.

You are what you eat – garbage in, garbage out.

A woman must know twice as much as her male counterpart to be considered equal.

Know the difference between aggressive and assertive.

Expect to have a "Good Hair Day" on the day you schedule a haircut.

Enjoy life – this is not a dress rehearsal.

Use a TO DO list.

Know how to be independent, know how to be part of a team, and know when to be which.

Don't try to lead all the time.

Take time to do nothing.

Don't be afraid to be alone. You must be your own best friend.

Self pity will keep your from moving on to better things.

Celebrate the accomplishments of others.

Decisions made in the light of morning beat most of those made in the dark of night.

You can like a man without loving him and you can love a man without liking him – but not for long.